THE GREAT SERUM RACE

Blazing the Iditarod Trail

ILLUSTRATED BY
JON VAN ZYLE

DEBBIE S. MILLER

BLOOMSBURY

NEW YORK   LONDON   OXFORD   NEW DELHI   SYDNEY

For all the heroic dogs that have saved lives. —J. V. Z.

For Jona and all our happy huskies. —D. M.

Many thanks to those who offered valuable research assistance: Laura Samuelson of the Carrie M. McLain Memorial Museum in Nome, Rose Speranza and Peggy Asbury of the University of Alaska's Rasmuson Library Archives, and staff at the Cleveland Museum of Natural History and the Iditarod Race Museum in Wasilla. A special thanks to Jon and Jona Van Zyle, Annette McDonald, Al John, Jane Haigh, Richard Burmeister, Pete Bowers, and Candy Waugaman. Last, I'm grateful to Ingeborg MacMillan, who knew Togo and Balto as puppies and shared her stories of early life in Nome.

First published in the United States of America in 2002 by Walker Books for Young Readers, an imprint of Bloomsbury Publishing, Inc.
First paperback edition published in 2006
www.bloomsbury.com

Bloomsbury is a registered trademark of Bloomsbury Publishing Plc

For information about permission to reproduce selections from this book, write to Permissions, Bloomsbury Children's Books, 1385 Broadway, New York, New York 10018. Bloomsbury books may be purchased for business or promotional use. For information on bulk purchases please contact Macmillan Corporate and Premium Sales Department at specialmarkets@macmillan.com

Library of Congress Cataloging-in-Publication Data available upon request
ISBN-10: 0-8027-8811-4 (hardcover)
ISBN-10: 0-8027-8812-2 (reinforced)
ISBN-10: 0-8027-7723-6 (paperback)
ISBN-13: 978-0-8027-7723-2 (paperback)

The illustrations for this book were created in acrylic on Masonite
Book design by Maura Fadden Rosenthal/Mspace
Printed in China by C&C Offset Printing Co., Ltd., Shenzhen, Guangdong
20 19 18 17 16 15 14 13 12

All papers used by Bloomsbury Publishing, Inc., are natural, recyclable products made from wood grown in well-managed forests. The manufacturing processes conform to the environmental regulations of the country of origin.

TOGO *(courtesy of Ingeborg MacMillan)*

INTRODUCTION

In the eyes of his master, Togo was a rascal. The eight-month-old Siberian husky nipped at other dogs, jumped out of windows, and chased after reindeer. It was no surprise when Leonhard Seppala drove his dog team to deliver supplies to a mining camp near Nome, Alaska, without the mischievous Togo.

At first Togo didn't mind being left behind. But that night a blizzard raged through Nome and he decided to escape. He sprinted across the dog yard and leaped over a seven-foot-high wire fence. As he hurled his body forward, the fence snagged his leg. Togo yelped for help. A caretaker ran outside to find Togo hanging upside down. The caretaker released him, and the determined husky dashed off into the snowstorm with a gashed leg.

Togo ran thirty-three miles through the blizzard and eventually found Leonhard the following morning. Amazed by Togo's strength and determination, Leonhard mended his cut leg and let him join the team. He discovered that Togo pulled harder than his other dogs and was a natural born leader. With boundless energy Togo ran seventy-five miles on his first day in the harness. After Leonhard delivered the mining supplies, the free-spirited husky led the team on the return trip to Nome.

In the coming years, Togo would run tens of thousands of miles with Leonhard, winning dog races and hauling supplies. But Togo's greatest run of all occurred when the town of Nome desperately needed help one winter.

On a dusky January afternoon in 1925, Dr. Welch walked quickly toward the outskirts of Nome. Sled dogs howled from their yards. Outside a small cabin, a worried Inupiat Eskimo mother greeted the doctor. She led him into her home where two small children lay in bed, struggling to breathe.

"Can you open your mouth?" Dr. Welch asked the three-year-old boy.

The weak child tried to open his mouth, but it was too painful for his swollen throat. His fever was extremely high. Dr. Welch comforted the mother and children, but there was little he could do. The next day, both children died.

Soon after, another girl, Bessie Stanley, was miserable with the same symptoms. But this time, Dr. Welch could examine Bessie's throat. He immediately recognized the symptoms of diphtheria. Poor Bessie would not live through the night.

Diphtheria. Dr. Welch had not seen a case in twenty years. This fast-spreading disease could wipe out the entire community of more than 1,400 people. Dr. Welch immediately met with the city council and recommended a quarantine. The schools and other public places were closed. Community leaders told people to stay in their homes.

There was only one way to fight diphtheria. The town needed a supply of antitoxin serum. Dr. Welch sent out a desperate plea for help by radio telegraph. The message soon reached Governor Bone in Juneau and other important officials. Newspapers across the nation picked up word that the historic gold rush town needed emergency help.

The nearest supply of serum was at a hospital in Anchorage, 1,000 miles away, across a snowbound wilderness. Officials considered flying the serum to Nome, but it was too dangerous to operate open cockpit planes in extreme-cold temperatures. In those days, planes were used only during the summer. Nome was an icebound port, so boats were not an option. The serum could travel partway by train, and then the only safe means of transport was by sled dog team.

On January 26, an Anchorage doctor carefully packed the glass bottles of serum for the long journey. The bottles had to be protected to keep the serum from freezing. He gave the twenty-pound bundle to the conductor at the train station. Soon, steam engine 66 began to chug its way north to Nenana, the closest railroad link to Nome. Nenana lay nearly 300 miles away, beyond the tallest mountains of North America.

On the frozen Tanana River, five-year-old Alfred John could hear the distant roar of the steam engine. His Athabaskan Indian family lived in a cabin near the train station in Nenana. Although it was late at night and nearly fifty degrees below zero, Alfred and his mother bundled up in their warmest caribou legskin boots and fur-lined parkas and walked to the station to greet the train.

As they waited by the tracks in the moonlight, Alfred watched the huge locomotive hiss steam into the frozen sky and slow to a screeching halt. He saw men unload the freight, and the conductor hand the serum package to Bill Shannon. Bill was the first of twenty mushers to carry the serum in a dog team relay to Nome. These brave men and their best dogs would travel nearly 700 miles on a snow-packed mail trail.

B ill covered the serum with a bear hide and lashed it to the sled. His strongest team of nine malamutes barked and were anxious to move. Just before midnight on January 27, Bill waved good-bye to Alfred and shouted to his dogs. *Swoosh!* Into the winter night, the dog team sped toward Tolovana, the first relay stop some fifty-two miles away.

Bill knew every turn of the trail. Like many of the mushers, his regular job was to transport mail and freight with his dog team. Traveling long distances in the extreme cold was a dangerous challenge. If the dogs ran too fast and breathed too deeply, they could frost their lungs. When the team reached bitter-cold stretches along the river, Bill slowed his dogs to protect them. He often ran behind the sled to keep himself warm.

Hundreds of miles away, Togo leaned into his harness and waited patiently for Leonhard Seppala to position Scotty and the other huskies. Togo, now twelve years old, was a proven leader for one of the strongest dog teams in the world. Leonhard, dressed in his warmest squirrel parka, sealskin pants, and reindeer mukluks, had carefully chosen twenty of his best dogs. Officials had asked the famed Norwegian musher to intercept the serum at Nulato, a village located halfway between Nome and Nenana.

Jingle, jangle—the bells on Leonhard's sled rang as the team rounded the corner. There were so many dog teams in Nome that mushers were required to carry bells to warn pedestrians. Togo led the team down Front Street while friends wished them good luck.

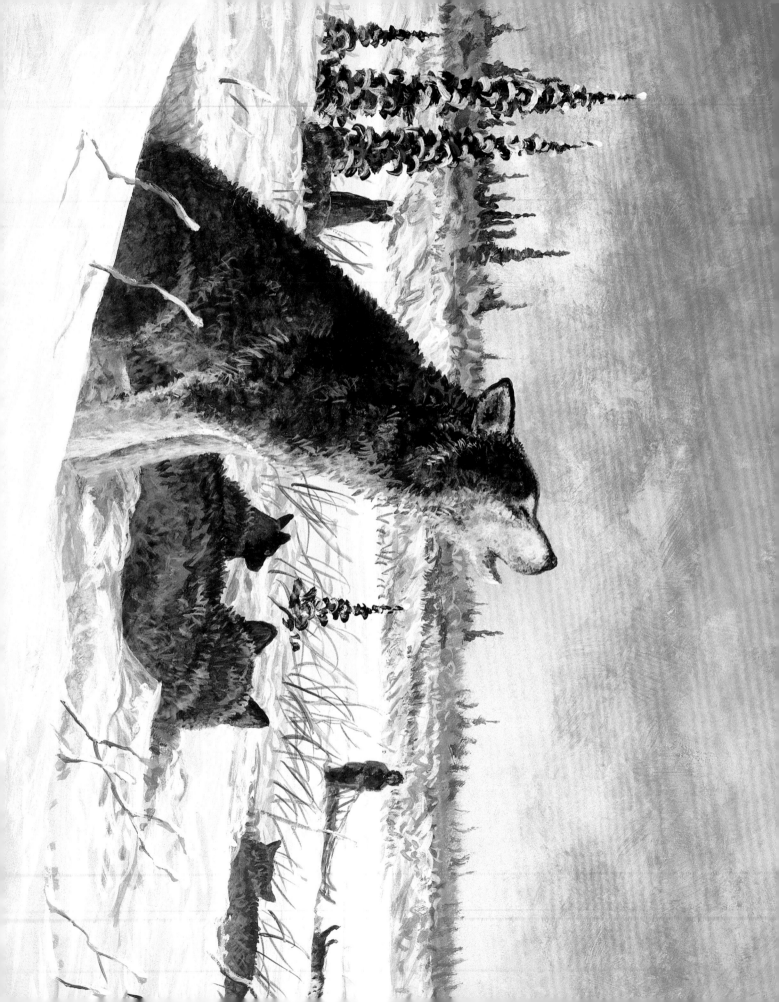

In Tolovana, Edgar Kalland, the twenty-year-old Athabaskan Indian mail driver, ate breakfast and waited anxiously for Bill Shannon. The Tolovana Roadhouse was a favorite rest stop for Edgar. Outside the roadhouse, Edgar's dogs pricked up their ears, and some began to howl. Bill's team drew closer.

The team looked exhausted when their frosted faces came into view. Two of the dogs would later die from frozen lungs. Following the doctor's instructions, Bill carefully removed the serum. He hurried into the roadhouse to warm the container and prevent the serum from freezing. As the two men talked about the weather, Edgar put on three pairs of socks and his boots.

Once the serum warmed, Edgar took off for Manley Hot Springs with his team of seven dogs. The thirty-one-mile trip to the next relay point was brutally cold. Temperatures fell to fifty-six degrees below zero. At one point the dogs had to wade through slushy overflow, a place where the river seeped through a crack in the ice. When the team reached Manley Hot Springs, the dogs could barely lift their ice-crusted legs. Edgar's mitts were frozen stiff to the sled handle. A roadhouse worker poured a kettle of hot water over the mitts to melt the ice and free Edgar's hands.

The relay continued from musher to musher, roadhouse to roadhouse, with teams pushing west through the biting cold. At each relay point, the mushers warmed the serum over wood-fired stoves. Following the winding rivers, the teams covered an average of thirty miles each, at a speed of six or seven miles per hour. The mushers traveled around the clock, usually by moonlight or twilight. In the middle of Alaska's winter, only a few hours of sunshine fell on the teams each day.

When the twelfth dog team headed for the village of Nulato, waves of northern lights flowed across the sky. Musher Charlie Evans faced the coldest temperatures at sixty-four degrees below zero. He wrapped the serum in a rabbit skin robe for extra protection. Charlie's nine-dog team moved slowly. Near open stretches of water on the Yukon River, a layer of eerie ice fog blanketed the valley. The ice fog, a mist of ice particles, was so dense that Charlie could barely see his wheel dogs, the ones closest to the sled. The experienced dogs followed the trail by scent rather than sight.

Nearing Nulato, two of the dogs moved stiffly and dragged their paws. The skin around their groin area was beginning to freeze. Charlie stopped the team and gently loaded the poor dogs into the sled. In their struggle to save the lives of Nome's residents, these two dogs would fall victim to the deadly weather.

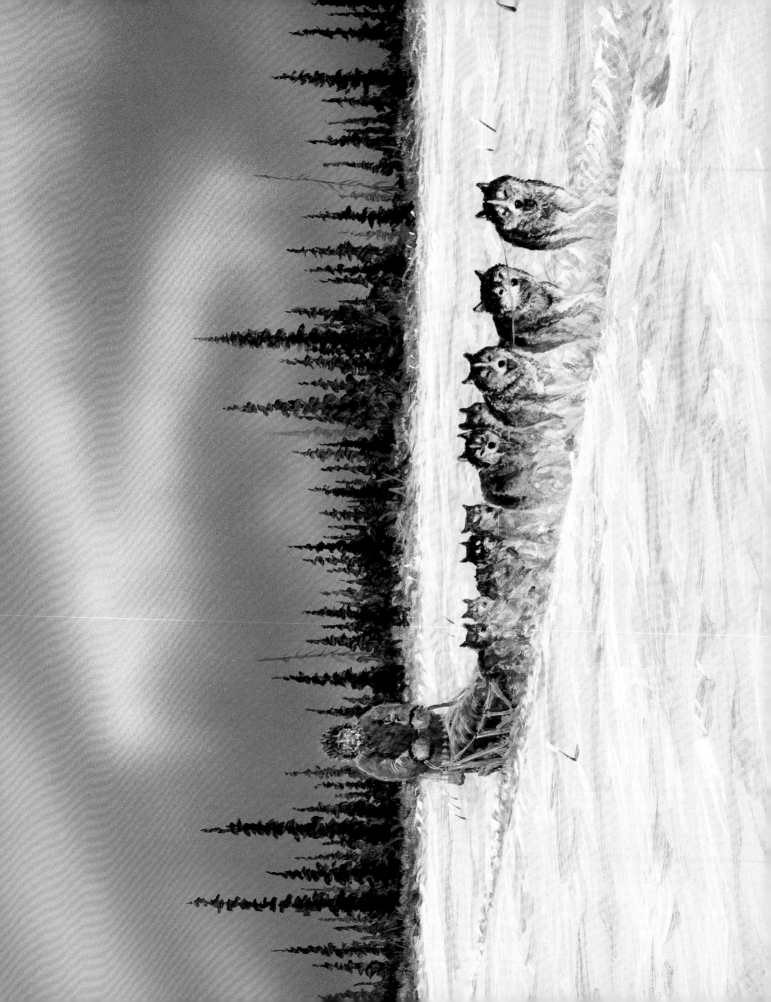

When the team reached the halfway point, conditions in Nome had grown worse. Five people had died from the disease, and more than twenty cases had been diagnosed. Another thirty people were suspected of having diphtheria. Newspapers across the country reported Nome's plight and the progress of the serum run.

The relay teams pressed onward. Togo and team worked their way east to intercept the serum. When Leonhard passed villages, he told residents about the epidemic and advised them to stay away from Nome. As the team approached the village of Shaktoolik, Togo picked up the scent of another dog team and sprinted forward. Leonhard could see a musher in the distance trying to untangle his string of dogs.

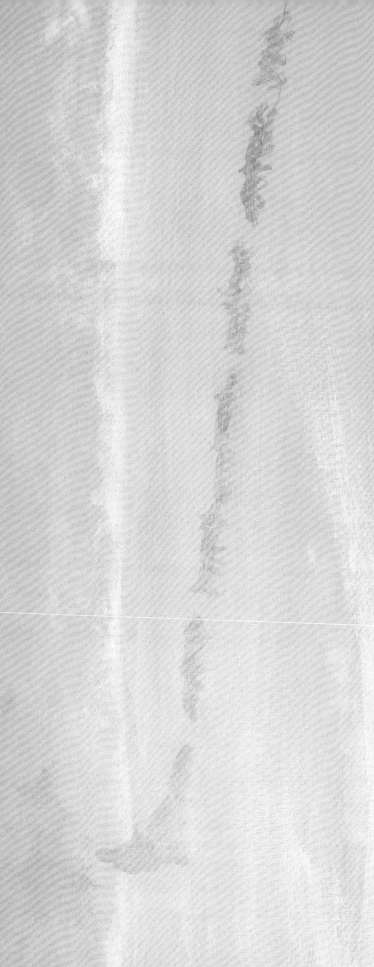

"On by!" Leonhard shouted to Togo.

Togo followed the familiar directions and steered the team away from the confusion.

"Serum—turn back!" shouted Henry Ivanoff, one of the relay mushers.

In the howling wind Leonhard barely heard the words. Luckily, he looked over his shoulder to see the musher waving frantically at him. Leonhard was surprised to see the relay team. After he set out for Nulato, twenty more mushers were chosen to travel short relays to speed up the serum run. Out in the wilderness, Leonhard had no idea that his rendezvous point was now 130 miles closer.

"Gee!" Leonhard yelled to Togo.

Togo gradually turned right and the swing dogs helped pull the sled toward the waiting team. The two men greeted each other briefly, shouting in the gale. Within minutes Leonhard had secured the serum package to his sled and instructed Togo to head home.

Togo and his teammates had traveled more than forty miles that day with the wind at their backs. Now the fierce gale blew in their faces with thirty below zero temperatures. Blowing snow plastered the team as they approached Norton Bay. Leonhard considered the risks. If they crossed the frozen bay, the sea ice might break up in the powerful gale. They could be stranded from shore on drifting ice. If they skirted the bay on land, the trip would take much longer. Leonhard thought of the children in Nome who were suffering from the disease. He decided to take the shortest route and cross the treacherous sea ice.

Leonhard believed that Togo could lead the team across twenty miles of frozen sea. As they pressed into the wind the dogs hit slick stretches of glare ice. They slipped, fell, and struggled to move forward. But mile after mile, Togo kept his course through the wall of wind. At day's end, Togo picked up the scent of food that drifted from the Inupiat sod house at Isaac's Point. After traveling eighty-four miles, they rested for the night. The dogs devoured their rations of salmon and seal blubber.

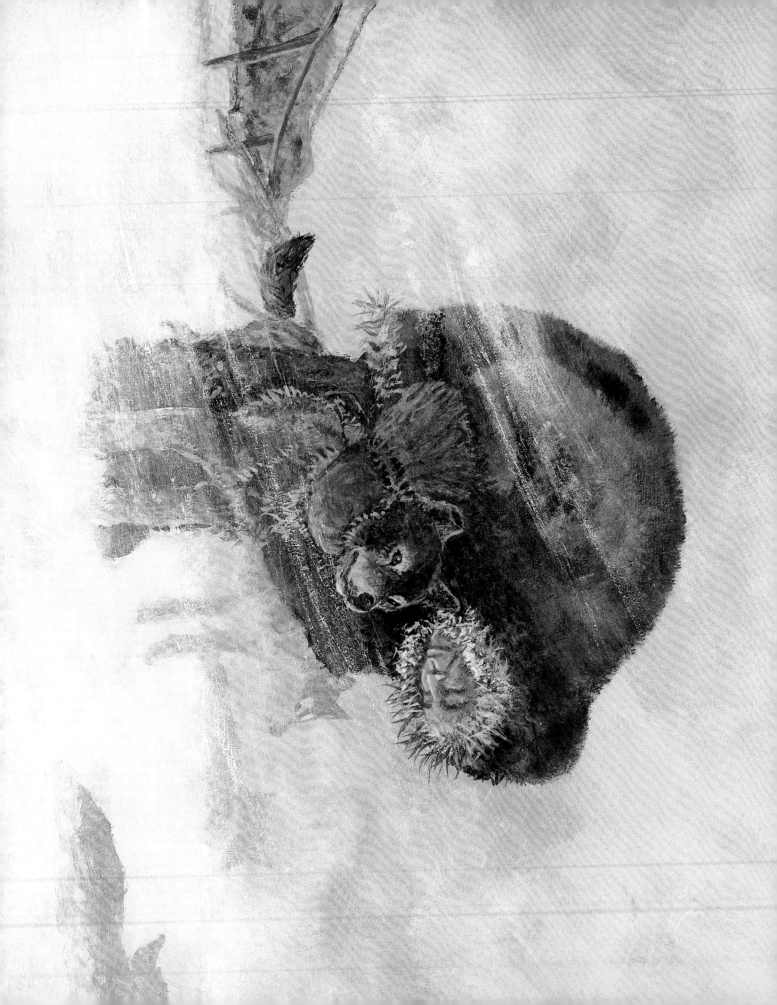

The following morning, Leonhard discovered that the previous day's trail had vanished. The ice had broken up and drifted out to sea. Worried about the unstable conditions, Leonhard decided to hug the shoreline for safety.

Togo led the way toward Dexter's Roadhouse in Golovin, about fifty miles away. Along the coast, the wind's force became unbearable. Blowing snow blasted the dogs' faces like buckshot. Some of the dogs began to stiffen up. Leonhard stopped the sled and gently massaged the freezing muscles of Togo, Scotty, and the others. When they finally reached Golovin, the dogs collapsed and buried their ice-coated faces beneath their tails. Togo and team had traveled farther than any other relay team.

Now it was another dog's turn to lead a fresh team of seventeen malamutes to Bluff, the final relay point. With a shout from musher Charlie Olson, lead dog Jack charged off into the blowing snow. After struggling through four hours of whiteout conditions, the experienced leader faintly heard a dog barking through the gale.

It was Balto.

At Bluff, Balto and Fox waited for Gunnar Kaasen to adjust the leather harnesses and secure the serum package. Then the pair of leaders heard their musher's shout through the raging wind. Balto and Fox led the strong team of thirteen huskies into the swirling snow. Mile after mile, they trotted steadily toward Nome. During the final leg of the run, the wind assaulted them. A violent gust flipped the sled over, and the dogs went flying.

Gunnar struggled to his feet against the might of the wind. After he fought to untangle the dogs, he checked the sled to make sure the serum was securely fastened. Gunnar felt the bottom of the sled in disbelief. The serum package was gone!

In the dark, he crawled around the sled. Since he couldn't see his surroundings, he took off his mitts and felt through the snow with his bare hands. After more than 600 hard-won miles and twenty teams risking their lives, could it be that the serum was lost forever?

Panicked, Gunnar ran his numb hands across windswept bumps of snow. All he could do was hope. Suddenly, he felt something hard. It was the serum! His frostbitten fingers struggled to tie the package onto the sled. Then the wind-battered team ran off.

They struggled on through the night. With less than twenty miles remaining, two of the dogs ran stiffly and appeared to be freezing. Gunnar anchored the sled and put rabbit-skin covers on the dogs to protect their undersides from frostbite.

Through the darkness, Balto and Fox smelled familiar scents. At last the exhausted team reached Nome. They drove into town as most people slept through the blizzard. When Gunnar knocked on the door, Dr. Welch greeted him with a stunned face. How could a musher and team have fought their way through such a storm?

With stiff hands, Gunnar gave the shocked but thankful doctor the life-saving serum.

Twenty brave mushers and more than 160 strong dogs traveled hundreds of miles in the worst conditions. The incredible relay took less than six days. Four dogs perished and several others grew lame because of the lethal weather. Yet their struggle saved many lives in Nome.

One month after the epidemic first began, the quarantine was lifted. The schools reopened and children hugged their old friends. The whole town celebrated by holding a dance and watching a movie at the theater. Togo, Scotty, Balto, Fox, Jack, and all the other dogs were true heros.

THE SERUM RUN MUSHERS

The mushers of the serum run represented a diversity of people living in Alaska. Several of them were Athabaskan Indians, others were Yupik Eskimos, and some were pioneers of Russian, Norwegian, or Irish ancestry. The mushers received between thirty and forty dollars for their heroic efforts, and they were honored with medals and special citations from Governor Bone.

Five days after the serum arrived in Nome, a second batch of serum was transported to Nome by dog teams. Some of the same mushers raced across Alaska in severe weather. All of the mushers from both serum runs have since died. Alfred John, the Athabaskan boy who watched Bill Shannon leave Nenana with the serum, is in his eighties and still lives in Nenana.

These are the mushers from the first serum run, the relay segment that they ran, and the distance they covered:

Musher	Relay segment	Distance covered
Bill Shannon	Nenana to Tolovana	52 miles
Edgar Kalland	Tolovana to Manley Hot Springs	31 miles
Dan Green	Manley Hot Springs to Fish Lake	28 miles
Johnny Folger	Fish Lake to Tanana	26 miles
Sam Joseph	Tanana to Kallands	34 miles
Titus Nikolai	Kallands to Nine Mile Cabin	24 miles
Dave Corning	Nine Mile Cabin to Kokrines	30 miles
Harry Pitka	Kokrines to Ruby	30 miles
Bill McCarty	Ruby to Whiskey Creek	28 miles
Edgar Nollner	Whiskey Creek to Galena	24 miles
George Nollner	Galena to Bishop Mountain	18 miles
Charlie Evans	Bishop Mountain to Nulato	30 miles
Tommy Patsy	Nulato to Kaltag	36 miles
Jackscrew	Kaltag to Old Woman Shelter	40 miles
Victor Anagick	Old Woman Shelter to Unalakleet	34 miles
Myles Gonangnan	Unalakleet to Shaktoolik	40 miles
Henry Ivanoff	Rendezvous with Seppala near Shaktoolik	
Leonhard Seppala	Nome to Shaktoolik (without serum)	170 miles
	Shaktoolik to Golovin	91 miles
Seppala's total miles		261 miles
Charlie Olson	Golovin to Bluff	25 miles
Gunnar Kaasen	Bluff to Nome	53 miles
		674 miles Total miles
		About 5-1/2 days Total time

Heroic Dogs of the Serum Run

More than 160 dogs worked together in the relay run to save Nome from the diphtheria epidemic. Each of the dogs on the 20 teams played an important role in bringing the serum hundreds of miles to the isolated community.

After the serum run, Balto received the most recognition and became a symbol for all the dogs that risked their lives to save the people of Nome. Balto's team starred in a short film about the serum run, and a statue of Balto was erected in New York City's Central Park in 1925. Balto drew the most attention because he and Fox led their team on the final relay leg. Fox was not mentioned because a reporter in Nome preferred the name "Balto" as a dog name for his news story.

Leonhard Seppala owned Balto and Togo, and he was troubled that Balto received so much fame, while Togo, his strongest leader and racer, received little recognition.

Both Togo's and Balto's teams toured the United States after the serum run. Shortly before his death, Togo was formally recognized at Madison Square Garden in New York City in front of 20,000 spectators. Arctic explorer Captain Roald Amundsen gave Togo a gold medal and spoke of all the dog's achievements, including his role in the serum run. After Togo died in Maine in 1929 at age sixteen, his body was mounted, and he was returned to Alaska in 1983. Today Togo resides at the Iditarod Race Headquarters in Wasilla.

Seppala eventually sold Balto's serum run team to a movie producer. After a number of Hollywood appearances, Cleveland businessman George Kimble discovered that Balto and team were ill and mistreated at a Los Angeles museum. Kimble established a Balto Fund and schoolchildren and other groups in Cleveland, Ohio, collected more than $2,000 to buy Balto's team and bring them to their city's zoo to receive proper care. Thousands of people visited the team at the Brookside Zoo. Balto died in 1933 at age fourteen, and his body is mounted and housed at the Cleveland Museum of Natural History.

IDITAROD TRAIL SLED DOG RACE

Every March, the Iditarod Trail Sled Dog Race commemorates the 1925 serum run to Nome. Today's race follows some of the same route used by the serum run mushers, along the historic Iditarod Trail.

The Iditarod Trail Sled Dog Race begins in Anchorage and ends in Nome, more than a thousand miles away. It is the longest sled dog race in the world. Just finishing the race is considered a great accomplishment.

For many years, Leonhard Seppala was recognized as the Iditarod's honorary musher because of his legendary racing record, his role in the serum run, and his enthusiasm and love for dog mushing. Seppala died in 1967 at the age of ninety. A new high school in Nome is named after him.

For more information about the Iditarod Trail Sled Dog Race and the serum run, visit www. iditarod.com

SELECTED SOURCES

Beck, Tom. Taped interviews with dog mushers Edgar Nollner, Charlie Evans, Bill McCarthy, and Edgar Kalland. Iditarod Trail Project Oral History Program, Bureau of Land Management, 1980. University of Alaska Fairbanks Archives.

Jones, Tim. Dog Heroes: True Stories about Extraordinary Animals Around the World. Seattle: Epicenter Press, 1995.

Mattson, Sue. Iditarod Fact Book: A Complete Guide to the Last Great Race. Seattle: Epicenter Press, 2001.

Murphy, Claire Rudolf, and Jane Haigh. Gold Rush Dogs. Anchorage: Alaska Northwest Books, 2001.

Rennick, Penny, ed. "Dogs of the North." Alaska Geographic 14, no. 1 (1987).

Rennick, Penny, ed. "The Iditarod." Alaska Geographic 14, no. 4 (2001).

Seppala, Leonhard. Seppala, Alaskan Dog Driver. Edited by Elizabeth Ricker. Boston: Little, Brown, 1930.

Sherwonit, Bill. Iditarod: The Great Race to Nome. Seattle: Sasquatch Books, 2002.

Thompson, Raymond. "Seppala's Saga of the Sled Dog." 2 vols. Manuscript, University of Alaska, Fairbanks, n.d.

Ungermann, Kenneth A. The Race to Nome: Alaska's Heroic Race to Save Lives. New York: HarperCollins, 1993.

LEONHARD SEPPALA WITH DOG TEAM. HIS BELOVED LEADER, TOGO, IS ON THE FAR LEFT. [courtesy of Ingeborg MacMillan]